MULTIPLE SCLEROSIS

MULTIPLE SCLEROSIS

A BITTER BATTLE WITH AN UNINVITED PARTY GUEST

A MEMOIR BY
SIERRA HAIRSTON

TIMELY FOUNTAIN/McLeansville, NC

Cover design: Damien Mayfield, DamienMayfield.com
Editing and interior design: HallagenInk.com

ISBN (Paperback): 979-8-9868485-0-1
ISBN (e-Book): 979-8-9868485-1-8

Printed in the United States of America

To Evelyn Hairston

*To the woman who wholeheartedly saved my life
by showing me the power of love, repentance, forgiveness,
sacrifice, and believing in God and myself.
Thank you, Mom*

Contents

1

The Beginning of a New Beginning

My story is complicated but simple. I never thought of myself as a secure and resilient person. I felt more like someone who went through the motions and storms of life. But isn't it funny how some storms in life can't be forgotten and pushed aside? Well, welcome to life. No, welcome to divine purpose.

I can reflect on many challenges I had in my life that I felt defeated and perceived as failures. What is my story? A tale of self-defeat and long-suffering that introduced me to self-discovery and acceptance. I intend not to have a pity party with balloons and cake but to highlight an encounter with a guest who arrived at my party with no invite. Who is the guest? How did you meet? Well, my friend, it's a long story, but come along. Let's talk.

I was born in the summer of July 1990 in the city of Greensboro, North Carolina. In 1997, my parents moved my sister and me to a small country town called Gibsonville, North Carolina. So, I grew up as a country girl.

Growing up, I considered myself to be healthy. I never spent a day in the hospital as a child or teenager. I was an overweight child but not obese. I had cavities due to overindulging in my snack cakes, candy bars, and sodas. I had typical seasonal allergies, flus, and colds. I dealt with a short battle of bronchitis in middle school. I did notice that as I developed into a teenager, I had an overgrowth of hair on my upper lip, neck, chin, and arm areas compared to the other girls my age. But none of those problems affected my overall health or functioning.

At the age of fourteen, a simple prayer changed my life forever. I had an encounter with God that would warn me of a series of events that would significantly impact my life. During that time, my family and I had settled at a church home. I started to take my relationship with God more seriously and began praying more. I discovered my gift of liturgical dance and became the dance ministry leader. I also assisted my mother, a missionary president at the church, with mission work in the church and community.

In prayer, one night, a voice that I call the Holy Spirit informed me that my life would be a great testimony, and I needed to start reading the book of Job in the Bible to strengthen my faith. I did not understand at the time, but I managed to read the book of Job. I was still young and did not understand the significance of my prayer, but I always felt that my life would be different. When I reflect on my teenage years after that prayer, I recall experiencing sharp pin and needle pains in my legs at night while sleeping in my bed from fourteen to seventeen. Nevertheless, I still had no concern about my health because those symptoms only happened sometimes at night, and I assumed it was part of my normal growth and development.

Take Notes

After graduating from Northeast Guilford High school in 2008, I attended Guilford Technical Community College (GTCC). While at GTCC, I still considered myself healthy. I had occasional headaches and everyday stress. I pushed through my classes and actively participated in a student transfer organization and campus activities. I still had moments when I experienced symptoms of pins and needles sticking in my legs at night while sleeping.

In 2010, I was texting my friend on my cell phone. I loved that phone because the phone could convert into a qwerty keyboard that slid out. While texting my friend one day, I noticed my right thumb was moving involuntarily. My thumb appeared to move side to side. Feeling concerned, I showed my mother my thumb. We were both perplexed, but we assumed it was because I texted too much and drank too many sodas. My thumb moved involuntarily for about thirty minutes. My mother told me to take notes and monitor my finger to see if it moved again. My mother also encouraged me to give my hand a break, talk on the phone to my friend, and limit the number of caffeine drinks I drank in a week.

I had several more incidents of my thumb moving involuntarily. When I was at home, I showed my mother, and I remember her telling me one day, "Sierra, I do not know what is going on with your thumb; it does not seem normal." My mother gave me another short lecture about talking to my friends on the phone more and drinking less soda. My mother did tell me if my finger continues to move involuntarily, I may want to go to my primary care physician for an assessment.

I seldom experienced nerve pain symptoms such as numbness in my left arm and sensitivity on my left side throughout my time at community college. I remember constantly grabbing my left arm because it felt weak at times. I regularly attended my annual physical exams and went to my primary care physician several times to address numbness and weakness in my left arm and leg, but my health exam cleared. The only medication prescribed to me was to address my iron deficiency anemia and acid reflux. My nerve pain symptoms continued to happen randomly.

Still, I continued pushing through my courses and successfully graduated from GTCC with my Associate of Arts in Pre-Social Work in May 2011. I felt incredibly proud of myself for completing a program and believed GTCC equipped me with a good work ethic and discipline that I needed to transfer to a university and graduate. I got accepted into my dream university North Carolina Agricultural and Technical State University (NC A&T SU), and life was good.

Work Hard, Play Later

Once I got into NC A&T SU, it was full speed ahead. My first semester started in August 2011. I was focused, my grades were good, and I was determined to graduate with honors and

4

possibly attend graduate school. I did not get involved in sororities, drinking, or going to the club trying to socialize. I lived on campus for my first semester in Barbee Hall. I soon realized that my maturity and focus level did not match the carefree attitude of freshman and sophomores leaving home for the first time. The upperclassmen had already formed their groups of friends. I found myself being in the library studying or doing my homework for hours, getting dinner, and going to my dormitory hall to rest. I felt like the old lady on campus and was lonely. I spoke with my mother and decided to move back home to save money and have some company. When I moved back home, I continued to focus on my schoolwork.

I did not mind commuting from school to campus, and I enjoyed eating my mother's home-cooked meals after a long day of school. It was not always easy living in the household, but God pulled me through and allowed me to persevere and get through each semester. My numbness and leg pain symptoms came back in 2012, and I noticed my symptoms lasted longer.

I continued to dance through my high school and college years. My family and I joined a new church, and I became a member of the dance ministry. Sometimes while dancing, I experienced horrible back pain and weakness in my legs, but I still managed to keep my balance and not fall. One dance practice in 2012, I fell off the stage in the sanctuary after losing my balance while doing a series of dance turns. Everyone in the dance practice was in shock. While on the floor, I had fellow dancers quickly pick me up off the floor and ask me how I was doing. I was embarrassed. Some fellow dancers laughed and chuckled once they found out I did not seriously injure myself. I joined in the laughter to save face, but in the back of my mind, I knew that I should have had better control of my legs and back, and it did not seem normal.

I began to have noticeable changes to my health. I experienced moments when I could not swallow entirely without feeling like I had food stuck in my throat. I started to experience chest tightness and numbness in my left arm that mimicked a heart attack. My acid reflux seemed to intensify. I had unusual fatigue. I went to my primary care physician (PCP) Dr. Smith to address my concerns, but my doctor dismissed my symptoms each time. It seemed to me that my doctor had too many patients to be attentive or concerned.

Nevertheless, I pushed through and continued my undergraduate studies. I would not let anything step in my way of graduating with my bachelor's degree. Despite my health challenges, I had the best experience at the university. I participated in campus engagement activities, transfer-student honor organization, community service, was inducted into several honor groups, traveled, and experienced the joys and woes of group work. The hard worked paid off, and I completed my courses and graduated from NC A&T SU with my Bachelor of Social Work degree in May 2013. To add the icing on the cake, I got accepted into graduate school at the Joint Master of Social Work Program (JMSW) with NC A&T SU and the University of North Carolina at Greensboro.

A Summer to Remember

I spent the summer relaxing and going on trips with my family before starting my first semester in graduate school in August 2013. I felt it was a great time to be young, educated, and living. I had no cares or worries. I felt a sense of entitlement and pride. In July 2013, I woke up with pain on the left side of my lower stomach. I thought it was gas and assumed the pain would pass. The pain did not go away. Days later, the pain intensified and I could barely walk. The only relief I would get was laying down on my right side. I went to my primary care physician and passionately expressed my symptoms and concerns. Dr. Smith seemed to be having a better day because she took the time to hear me out. She referred me to get a CT scan of my abdomen the same day.

The CT scan showed a cyst on my ovary. I was diagnosed with Polycystic ovary syndrome (PCOS). I felt shocked but not surprised because ovarian cysts ran in my family. I finally got my answer to why I always had an overgrowth of hair on my face and arms and irregular menstrual cycles. I took birth control to reduce my chances of developing more ovarian cysts. A few weeks after my appointment, my ovarian cyst ruptured when my menstrual cycle came on. I felt instant relief but knew that I would always have a history of ovarian cysts, and my chances of having more cysts were high. Still determined, I persevered and looked forward to graduate school in the fall.

The Big League

My first semester of graduate school began in August 2013. I soon learned that keeping up with deadlines and completing your work ahead of time was required to reduce unnecessary stress. I was a procrastinator and expected things to flow like milk and honey. I struggled with my time management and started to experience fatigue at a level that affected my ability to complete work promptly. My professors were firm but fair at the same time. Fortunately, my professors extended the deadline for some of our assignments because they knew that the students were still adjusting to the fast-paced graduate-level workload and balancing personal lives.

I was experiencing physical challenges already, but my mother noticed that my mental and emotional state was also wearing me down. As quickly as a grease fire can start on a stove with an unattended pan of grease, I began to have pain in my body. I began to feel a sharp pain in my stomach and nausea in October 2013. My stomach felt full all the time. The pain started to intensify and became unbearable. At times, I felt like I could barely walk, and I felt nauseated.

My sister and I planned a fun girl's day out, but a day of pleasure soon turned to pain. We decided to get some lunch at a local restaurant. We ordered our appetizers and entrees. We received our fried onion appetizer, and I enjoyed every bite. In the middle of eating the appetizer, my stomach started to turn for the worse. I felt nauseated and only took a few bites of my entree. I had pains in my upper abdomen and started to dry heave. We decided to leave the restaurant and go back home.

After my experience at the restaurant, I knew that I had no other option but to reach out to my primary care physician.

The following week, I called Dr. Smith and set up an appointment for a few days later to address my nausea and stomach pain. Dr. Smith examined my stomach and referred me to a gastroenterologist for further testing. I waited several weeks to be seen by the gastroenterologist because she had a full schedule.

Gastroenterologist Visit

My gastroenterologist, Dr. Fischer, was quick, sharp, and thorough. Within three minutes of the exam, she informed me that my gallbladder was the cause of my discomfort and pain, but further tests will confirm or deny the level of functioning of my gallbladder. I remember going to one of my exams with my sister. A nurse asked me if a particular event happened that made me go to the doctor. I told her I went to a restaurant, shared a fried onion appetizer with my sister, and became sick after eating it.

She instantly busted into a laugh and stated, "Oh my goodness, I don't mean to laugh, but it's always the fried onion appetizer. I have had multiple patients become sick after eating it, so I grew accustomed to people telling me about it. I guess the fried onion appetizer is the final straw."

My sister and I had a good laugh with the nurse. Several more tests determined that my gallbladder was operating at a low percentage, and I would need a cholecystectomy to remove it. The diagnosis came as a shock to my family and me. My life in graduate school slowly began to unravel. My stomach pains became intense, and I started having difficulty passing stool. I stayed constipated. I wondered to myself, *How did my life become so troubled in a matter of months?* I began to feel stressed and tired at a level that I had never felt before. I got behind on my assignments due to my deteriorating health. I had a moment at my internship that I had to excuse myself from the day treatment classroom because I felt horrible. I started to dry heave and could not keep water or anything down. I walked to my supervisor's office to inform her of my condition. My supervisor told me to go home and get some rest. She knew I was waiting for my surgery to be scheduled and worked with adjusting my hours. The only available surgery date was weeks before my semester ended.

The Joint Master of Social Work Program (JMSW) program had a meeting weeks before my scheduled surgery to discuss whether I could remain in the program due to unforeseen medical reasons. The JMSW program agreed to let me stay in the program, permitting that I complete all my papers and turn in any remaining work before the spring semester. I shared the news with some of my classmates, and they wished me all the best. I completed most of my exams and papers before my surgery. I received my cholecystectomy on December 3, 2013. Some classmates reached out to me to check in, but I was still healing from my surgery and emotionally broken. I needed time to myself, but I was looking forward to going back in January for the spring 2014 semester.

My surgery was successful, and I had the opportunity to rest and complete a paper before the new semester arrived. On the first day of the spring 2014 semester, I arrived on campus feeling better physically, but struggled with fear that something unexpected would happen again. When I walked into the classroom, I could tell that some of my classmates were shocked to see me back, but they were happy that I felt better. I received support from my professors and felt ready to start the spring semester even though I still felt uneasy.

Fake It till You Make It

My body felt better, and I believed I had time to begin the new semester with a clean slate. However, I did not feel one hundred percent because I was still experiencing fatigue and brain fog that affected my overall energy, concentration level, and quality of work. I also experienced challenges in my internships regarding health and time management, but I remained determined to finish my semester strong.

I was embarrassed and ashamed to tell my professors about what was going on. I kept pushing myself and turning in substandard work, hoping I would slide through the cracks. But eventually, they would find out. A fantastic professor (who taught me in the undergraduate social work and graduate school programs), brought me into his office one day and informed me that my writing quality had changed. I told him that the health challenges and adjusting to the graduate program workload affected my ability to be at my best. He encouraged me to keep going, allowed me to rewrite my paper, and I received an A. Another professor spoke with me to discuss concerns. He was a stand-up professor who gave all his students time to grow and fix their mistakes. He was firm but fair. I had the opportunity to complete a paper for his class.

A Near-Death Experience

One night around March 2014, I pulled an all-nighter to complete a paper due the following day. I knew I had to attend my internship the next day, about forty-five minutes away in Winston- Salem, North Carolina, but I thought I could handle it. The following morning, before I left home, my father asked if I wanted him to take me to my internship because I stayed up all night doing a paper. I told him that I would be fine. I enjoyed having my freedom driving and not being picked up at the internship by my parents like a young child. My pride got in the way of sound judgment. My father was hesitant to let me go, but told me if I needed anything to call him.

I told my father goodbye and left home around 7:30 am. I would total my car within minutes up the street on a country road. The only thing I remember is driving in my car and listening to gospel music with my eyes open. My car left the road fast, and I cried out to God to save my life. I attempted to put my foot on the brake and went out of control. I hit a ditch. A voice came to me and said, "Hold on to the steering wheel and don't let go." I held on to the steering wheel, my car flipped on its side, but it landed hard and safely on four wheels.

In shock, I looked around, and my car started to smoke. My driver's door bent in. I had just enough space to get out. I got my cellphone and jumped as fast as I could out of the car. A driver passing by saw my car smoking and asked if I needed any help. I told him I had just got in a car accident and told him to help me. I gave him my phone, and he called my father. My father arrived in five minutes. I thanked the Good Samaritan, and he waited with my father and me until the Sheriff's officer arrived to take the report.

My father was upset with the situation but was glad that I came out of the accident alive. I told my mother and she was disappointed in my lapse of judgment. She was also upset that she had just replaced the motor in my car, and now it was totaled. My mother expressed that she was not happy with my decision, but was thankful that God protected me from being seriously injured. From that day on, I never drove sleepy again.

I can say with confidence that God's grace allowed me to complete the graduate program. My determination paid off and I graduated with my Master of Social Work degree in May 2015 with a grade point average over 3.6. I also got inducted into a graduate-level social work honor society. I knew God gave me the grace to complete the JMSW program. My heart was full of gratitude for the promise that God kept. I was ready to start my journey. Well, at least I thought I had everything prepared to begin life. Buckle your seat belt, my friend. You are in for a wild story.

2

The Uninvited Guest

G raduating with my master's degree in social work made me feel like a warrior that slew a vicious dragon. I felt fulfilled and accomplished. After graduate school, I received a summer job at NC A&T SU as an administrative assistant. I enjoyed the summer job and even won an employee rookie of the year award. After the summer job ended, I chose to work at a community mental health center as a licensed clinical social work associate. My life—the party, as I call it—was going well. I welcomed in all the accomplishments and achievements. I thought my life was going at a good pace. I enjoyed dancing to the beat of my own drum. However, soon the drum would become silent, and the party would be interrupted.

The new job was not what I expected. It was hard work with a stressful environment. I went on home, school, and office visits throughout the day in three different counties, and it became too much for me to handle. I had difficulty with my time management and felt overwhelmed by the workload.

Sometime around November 2015, I remember making my last home visit to a new client's home who lived in a rural area. The client was not home, and I could not contact her on the cell phone. I lost my GPS signal after leaving the client's home. It was cold and rainy that day, and the sun was quickly setting. I forgot my cell phone charger at home, so my cell phone battery was low. I drove around in the dark for over an hour until I found a familiar street name to head back home.

I had an episode of feeling extremely dizzy and felt like I was going to pass out. I prayed to God the whole time and asked Him to give me the strength to make it home. I called my mother to inform her that I was feeling dizzy, but I was going to push through because I was almost home. My mother stayed on the phone with me until I got home. After that day, I started to experience an increase in health issues, including severe fatigue, dizziness, headaches, brain fog, and numbness and weakness in both arms and legs. To make a long story short, both the job and I parted ways in December 2015. It was a hard pill to swallow, but that was nothing compared to the series of events that would happen afterwards. I spent most of my days crying and regretting the decision I made choosing that job. I knew I needed to get my feet wet and work a social work job that would help build my skills before entering a specialty, but my pride and arrogance took over. I thought I was ready to embark on a journey of self-discovery, but immaturity and looking at a job to validate my self-esteem and status in the world made a fool out of me.

My health started to decline rapidly in January 2016.

The Party

I started to have more pain and weakness in both legs especially while laying down at night. This went on for several weeks. They were the same symptoms I experienced in high school and college. I thought the pain in my legs was coming from stress and not exercising. My mother had recently adopted a sweet nine-month-old chihuahua from the local animal shelter named Jack. He arrived in January 2016. I decided to start walking outside with Jack for about fifteen minutes a day to get exercise and reduce my stress.

My family and I went to a store one cold evening in February 2016. On our way home, I felt my legs getting numb and weak in the car. When we arrived back home and I walked out of the vehicle, something felt different. My legs felt stiff, like concrete bricks were holding down both feet. I barely made it to the backdoor without almost falling on the ground. I called out for my mother to help me. She helped me get in the backdoor, but my legs swung back and forth like a swinging pendulum. I almost fell on the floor, but my mother caught me in her arms and helped me get into the bed. Within fifteen minutes of the incident, both my legs went completely numb.

My mother's background as a registered nurse prompted her to do a reflex assessment on both my legs and feet to check for movement. My mother asked if I felt any sensation in my legs and feet during the evaluation, and I responded no. My mother put her hand over her head and said in a somber voice, "Oh my God, Oh my God." She told me that I would need to set up an appointment. She was careful not to assume or diagnose medical conditions without the proper medical tests. The next day, I called the primary care physician to set up an appointment.

I did not let that one incident stop me from driving to the store to get something to eat, so I went to the grocery store a few days later. I was feeling good enough to drive. My legs felt a little funny while driving, but it did not affect my ability to drive. When I got out of my car, I noticed that my right foot appeared to flop to the side like a fish. I could not believe what I was seeing. But I kept walking into the store.

I walked into the frozen food section and decided to jog in the aisle to see if my foot would flop again. As soon as I started jogging, my right foot spasmed and dropped to the side. I was shocked, so I cut my grocery store visit short, hurriedly grabbed some food, and left. I was able to drive myself home, but I had a gut feeling that something was not right with my legs.

Days later, my legs began to get weak, and I started to fall at home. I fell on the ground outside my home several times. Most times, my mother or father would be at home to help pick me up after I fell. I knew that my body was rapidly changing, and the wellness visit was necessary more than ever.

I finally had my assessment with my primary care physician, Dr. Smith, and she noticed that my right foot appeared weak and my gait was off. She referred me to a neurologist. In the weeks leading up to my visit with the neurologist, I wrote down the symptoms I was experiencing. My symptoms included headaches, vertigo, tingling and burning sensations in my feet, falling, temporary right foot weakness, weakness in my arms and legs, and fatigue. I was more convinced that my issues were neurological.

I lay on the sofa and cried out to God in anguish and pain. I asked Him to tell me what was going on with my body. I heard a soft voice tell me, you are sick, but you will be okay. I decided at that moment to ask God to please tell me the medical diagnosis. I felt led to go to the internet and search my symptoms in a database. The medical condition of multiple sclerosis (MS) appeared on the screen. My body felt numb, and disbelief came over me. Tears streamed down my face as I cried on the sofa. My dog Jack looked at me, walked over to the couch, and tried his best to comfort me by resting his head on my foot.

I informed my mother about what I thought my diagnosis might be when she came home from work, but she quickly encouraged me to wait for all tests to rule or rule out my medical condition before assuming anything, and pray.

A Lesson Learned through Nature

One morning in March 2016, I walked in my yard with my dog Jack. I was in sorrow and deep pain this day, realizing how much my life changed. My heart was full of grief and pain. Before I entered the gate after walking Jack into the house, I heard a voice that said, "Look at that tree behind you. What do you notice about this tree?"

I observed the large oak tree for about one minute, and I told the voice the tree is brown with no blooms, so the tree is dead for the season.

The voice told me, "Isn't this tree living? Just because you do not see any leaves on the tree does not mean that it is dead. The tree is alive, and its roots are strong. The roots and nutrients are keeping this tree alive. Sierra, just because your situation looks dead does not mean you are. You are very much alive. If you stay in me and my Word, I am the soil and nutrients that will keep you living."

Neurologist Visit

My older sister Mandesia drove me to the neurologist appointment on April 12, 2016. On our way, she gave me words of encouragement and asked me to pray. I entered the neurological center and was overwhelmed by seeing several middle-aged and older adults walking with walking aides and being pushed in wheelchairs by their caretakers. The neurologist Dr. Wood was a woman, nice, and had the best bedside manners. She conducted a neurological exam. She noticed that my gait was off as my foot slightly dragged across the floor and I wobbled while walking. I could not move my left index finger in a circular motion without my hand tremoring. My balance, coordination, and reflexes appeared not to be normal.

After the assessment, I asked the neurologist what it could be. The neurologist gently spoke and said, at this time, it looks like it may be multiple sclerosis based on your physical symptoms. Still, we do not know until we get some magnetic resonance imaging (MRI) tests done tomorrow. She informed me the MRI would scan my brain and spine for lesions, and if they are present, more additional tests will rule or rule out medical diagnosis.

My heart sank. I could see the shock on my sister's face. After the visit, my mother called to check-in. I did not speak on the phone much because I was shocked. My sister talked with our mother to fill her in on the details of the visit. My mother and sister told me to wait until the MRI and all tests were complete before assuming the worse. But I could not help but think the worse. I had a gut feeling that something would happen to change my life forever.

First MRI

My sister took me to my MRI appointment the next day on April 13, 2016. I remember feeling uneasy and nervous. Two friendly MRI technicians greeted me and asked a series of screening questions. I changed into my white patient gown and followed a technician into the mobile MRI scanner. I lay flat on my back on the MRI machine table and received an intravenous drip in my arm. I was given a pair of earplugs.

My MRI included both a scan with contrast and non-contrast to assess for abnormalities and medical conditions. A piece of specialized equipment that looked like a football helmet was placed over my head to scan my brain. When I got in the MRI machine, it was very tight. I could see why the technicians ask patients if they are claustrophobic. I remained calm and silently prayed. A voice came to me and told me that I would be okay and to relax. The technician gave me directions and checked in with me through a speaker located in the machine. I also had a handheld device that I could squeeze if I needed assistance. The sounds in the machine were loud and sounded like large lasers and clacking robots.

Throughout the MRI session, my head, especially on the right side, was burning like fire. I moved my head so much in one image set that the MRI technician had to retake images. When the MRI session was complete, both technicians carefully helped me step off the table. The head technician asked me again if I or any of my relatives have been diagnosed with MS. I told the technician no. The technician gently smiled and told me to take care of myself, and the neurologist will call me with the results. I felt relief after getting my MRI because I knew that soon I would find out what was causing my neurological symptoms.

A Day to Remember

It was a sunny afternoon in Gibsonville, NC, on April 14, 2016. The sun was setting nicely in the west, with sun rays shining beautifully through the blinds. I was sitting on the sofa having a conversation about life with my mother as she prepared dinner. I remember feeling anxious and worried most of the day because I was waiting to hear the results of the MRI exam I had yesterday.

"Mom, I'm not feeling well. I hope nothing is wrong."

My mother spoke in a calm voice, "Well, Sierra, we will have to wait for the results to come in and deal with it at that time."

About ten minutes later, I received a phone call from Dr. Wood. She gently explained to me that three brain lesions were present. The initial shock of hearing what she reported on my health blocked my mind from processing. I asked the doctor if she could speak to my mother. She told my mother about the MRI findings and that I would need to schedule the additional tests to confirm or rule out multiple sclerosis (MS).

I spoke back to Dr. Wood and scheduled an appointment for the following day to review the MRI results and to schedule more tests. We also arranged for a separate office visit with my mother. I took a deep breath and exhaled after I ended the call.

My mother told me she thought it might have been MS but did not want to say anything until test ruled or ruled out the diagnosis. My mother told me to remain positive because we would get through this situation.

I sat on the living room sofa in a state of disbelief with tears flowing down my cheeks. My mother said, "Why are you crying? We are going to have to take one day at a time."

My dad came in the door from work moments later. He noticed an awkward silence and said, "Is everything okay? Did you hear about your MRI results?"

I could not tell my dad at the time, so my mother told him what was going on. My dad looked concerned and asked about treatment. My mother let him know that more tests are required before treatment is selected.

My father replied, "Okay, baby, I hope you will be okay."

My mother said, "Sierra, I am going to have to tell your sister."

I knew telling my sister would be challenging because my sister is the one who took me to the neurologist for my initial assessment and MRI. She was concerned but remained optimistic until the results were final. My heart broke into a thousand pieces thinking about my sister's reaction. I begged my mother not to tell my sister because she was working a job and attending graduate school. I did not want to be a distraction. My mother told me it is essential to inform my sister because my health affects the family.

My mother walked outside to call my sister. My mother walked back into the house ten minutes later, handed the phone to me, and said, "Your sister wants to talk with you."

I took the phone, and I could tell she was crying because I heard her sniffing and her sad voice. My sister said she felt it might have been MS, but many people with MS can still live productive lives. She wanted me to get the remainder of the tests to confirm and start treatment. I felt more encouraged to face my new reality.

The following day I drove to the neurology center. As I waited in the waiting room, all I could think about was how much my life would change and how everyone would perceive me. I felt displaced and lost. I was the only Black, young, adult woman in the room full of older adults, at least forty years my senior, in wheelchairs and walking on canes. The nurse called me to the examination room, and completed check-in.

Dr. Wood entered the room with a gentle smile and politely greeted me. We reviewed my lab results, which came back normal. While we reviewed my MRI results, I could not believe that I was looking at my brain. The size and shape of the lesions amazed me. At first, I thought it might have been another person's MRI, but when I looked at the shape of the forehead, I knew there was no missing my distinct egg-shaped head.

I saw two lemon-sized lesions on the back of my brain and a grapefruit-sized lesion on the right side of my brain. She informed me that the grapefruit-sized brain lesion was in the thalamus part of my brain, responsible for sensory impulses and movements. The lesions on my thalamus can cause movement disorders, which explains why I had difficulty with my balance, coordination, and gait. She told me they would look closely to rule out other medical conditions because the grapefruit-sized lesion was in an area of the brain not common in MS patients. She informed me that I would have a lumbar puncture (LP) to confirm or rule out MS. I agreed to the test, and she left the office to schedule the appointment and prepare my summary visit documentation.

When she left, my head sunk in my chest, and I became overwhelmed with grief. She entered the room and saw my distress and hugged me. I felt comfort and support in a moment of helplessness. We discussed that my mother could come back to the office the following Monday.

I remember driving back home in silence. I had no music playing, and I managed to block everything out going on around me. I am thankful that I made it home safely. I came home and laid in bed feeling sad. I managed to eventually fall asleep as my eyes could not cry out any more tears.

Monday came, and I went back to the neurologist with my mother to discuss the MRI results and upcoming tests. My mother handled the appointment well. My mother was shocked to see the size of the lesions on my brain and curious about the lesion found in the thalamus. Dr. Wood informed us that if the lumbar puncture test reveals positive MS antibodies, they will call and refer me to the neurologist MS specialist who just came to the practice. She spoke highly of her new colleague and bragged that his patients loved him. She said that he offers more knowledge about MS than she could offer because he was a MS specialist.

She informed me to drink plenty of fluids, keep a regular sleep-wake schedule, eat healthy meals, not skip any meals, eat healthy snacks like fruits and nuts between meals, and exercise daily particularly in the form of walking twenty to thirty minutes a day if I could.

I had a lumbar puncture exam on April 20, 2016. I felt anxious. The doctor and nurse doing my test were both friendly. Before I took the test, they drew my blood for labs. I remember laying on the examination table with my back bent facing the doctor. I peeked behind me and saw that the needles going in my back were long. The doctor informed me that he was collecting my spinal fluid to check for MS anti-bodies and told me what to expect during the procedure. The doctor braced me for the needle injection and collected the spinal fluid quickly. The nurse held me close to keep me calm. The nurse asked me a few times if I was okay because I remained still and quiet. I responded with a head nod.

I experienced the worst headache in my life for days after. The headache was a common symptom patients had after the lumbar puncture test. Days later, I received a call from the nurse at the neurological center to inform me that my examination revealed that my official diagnosis was multiple sclerosis, and I would need to come into the office to discuss treatment options with the MS specialist. I knew officially that my life would never be the same.

Treatment

I met with my assigned neurologist, Dr. Hansen, on April 25, 2016. He would be responsible for helping me manage my MS symptoms and treatments. His specialty was MS, and he was known to have a vast knowledge of the disease and good rapport with his patients. He was an average height man with salt and pepper hair who carried himself with confidence and humility.

My mother and sister accompanied me to the appointment. We all reviewed my MRI brain scan and discussed the symptoms associated with my lesions and disease-modifying medications that would help slow down the disease progression. He informed me that I had the Relapsing-remitting MS (RRMS), and that researchers were still trying to discover the cause of MS and find a cure for it. I managed to block out some of the information he told me. Imagine how the famous American television character Charlie Brown's teacher Miss Othmar sounded talking to her students in class.

I did not know any Black people with MS except for the famous American comedian and actor Richard Pryor and American talk show host Montel Williams. I instantly became concerned when I thought about Richard Pryor because his symptoms progressed. It affected his mobility, and he was driving a mobility scooter. In the last photos I saw, Richard Pryor was being transported in a wheelchair by others. I was overwhelmed and scared, so I remained silent throughout the visit.

My mother and sister asked most of the questions regarding treatment. He could sense that I was tense and withdrawn. He asked if I had any concerns when it comes to treatment. I told him that my main concern was symptoms associated with the treatments. We discussed the available treatment options ranging from low-risk symptoms to high-risk symptoms. Finally, we talked about a subcutaneous injection treatment. The most common symptoms were flu-like symptoms, decrease white blood cell count, and redness at the injection site. My family and I decided to start with the subcutaneous injection treatment every two weeks. The neurologist gave me a form to fill out to enroll in the treatment program with the pharmaceutical company, and he informed me that representatives would be in contact with me soon. He encouraged me to keep a regular sleep-wake schedule, eat healthy meals, exercise daily when I could, and reduce my stress level. The overall visit went well, and I felt like I was working with an MS neurologist specialist who valued my health and treatment.

My family and I went on a family vacation in May, 2016, to a resort in Gatlinburg, Tennessee, a few days after my first meeting with my treatment neurologist. I did not have the best attitude and wanted to lie in bed. I felt doomed, like my life was over. Days later, a nurse educator from the pharmaceutical company reached out to me to ask me if I had any questions regarding the medication and to assist me with enrolling in the patient assistance program (a program used to help patients pay for their medication). I received calls from the pharmaceutical company and the insurance company regarding my medication approval and delivery status.

My mother and I talked to several representatives each day of the trip; I grew weary. I cried and did not want to do anything with my family on the trip. My mother knew I was being a butthead but remained civilized and told me firmly to get myself together because this would not disappear. My mother encouraged me to write down who I spoke to because we did not need any delays with the patient assistance program. I only wrote down some names and did not keep a detailed record.

The morning my family and I left, I decided to sit on the back porch of the resort. It was peaceful and away from everyone. I just wanted to be alone. I noticed a beautiful crystal-clear stream that flowed over large and small rocks.

A voice came to me and directed me to look at the creek. "Sierra, your life will be like a stream if you let me flow through you. I've come to give you life."

I smiled and said, "God. You will not even let me have a day to be angry without reminding me of your grace and power."

For several weeks, I went back and forth with the representatives to make sure my medication arrived. Still, the patient assistance program had to manually put an override in the system because the cost of my medication exceeded the price provided on the co-pay assistance card. I learned that I was not the only patient and needed to check in every few days to ensure that my medication would be approved and shipped. I probably would have received my medication early had I written down who I spoke with in a journal like my mother asked me to. It was incredibly stressful, and I learned it is essential to follow up with all parties involved, such as the health insurance company, patient assistance program, neurologist, and specialty pharmacy. It was a long and complicated process. I spent weeks talking to all the parties involved. But eventually, I was able to set up a shipment date with the specialty pharmacy, and days later, I received my medication through mail delivery in June.

Next, my mother and I set up a home visit with a nurse educator from the pharmaceutical company to learn how to inject the medication appropriately. The injection sites are the arms, legs, and stomach.

I remember my first injection: the needle was sharp, and it was painful. After my injection, I developed flu-like symptoms such as a fever, chills, body aches, and headaches. Days later, I had redness and pain at the injection site. My mother had to give me the injections because I was afraid to do them myself. I received most of my injections in the evening, so I could lie down on my bed to rest. Most times after receiving my injection, I would be awakened in the morning around two or three o'clock due to side effects.

I did not enjoy getting the injections because I would develop flu-like symptoms with every shot. Rotating the injection sites every two weeks between my arms, legs, and stomach became the norm. The worst area to get an injection was on both sides of my stomach because the needle was sharp, and I would have medium-sized bruises on my skin that itched. Finally, I learned that I had to medicate my body with acetaminophen to help me reduce my flu-like symptoms. The next few months would be an adjustment for my family and me, but we moved forward and continued to live our lives.

Getting Acquainted with the Uninvited Guest

As you know by now, the uninvited guest to my party was multiple sclerosis (MS). I feared that I would lose my youth and independence. I thought to myself, *Who would want to marry me now? What about me having children?*

In my early neurological appointments, I did not engage in the sessions as much. I asked and answered the bare minimum questions. My mother engaged more with my neurologist because I felt overwhelmed during my appointments. My neurologist always made sure he checked in with me not only with my physical health but my emotional health. He informed me about available resources and services in the community to assist me.

On most days I ignored my diagnosis, took my subcutaneous injections every two weeks, and tried to act normal. I asked my mother questions about MS, doctor appointments, and treatment. My mother often encouraged me to educate myself on how MS affects people, to learn about my treatment, and explore MS supportive services in the community, but I feared if I acknowledged MS, my life would be limited.

Not to mention, there were very few studies of how African Americans or Black people were affected by multiple sclerosis. However, as a black woman and a social worker, I understood some of the complex issues Black people faced in the community. Some examples of the challenges that I observed and personally experienced are the following: inadequate health care and services due to lack of resources and funds, lack of health education, transportation issues, poverty, employment challenges, conflict within the family, and distrust regarding taking medication and participating in research trials due to fear of mistreatment of their health.

I've seen the difficulties people faced having a certain health insurance that limits the services people receive and adds people to a wait list that is longer for certain medical services. Unfortunately, some people even succumb to their health issues. My mother made sure my health was her priority and I received a good health insurance plan that paid for me to have access to different treatments and services.

What is Multiple Sclerosis?

According to the National Institute of Neurological Disorders and Stroke, multiple sclerosis (MS) is a disabling neurological disease in which the immune system cells used to protect people from the unhealthy cells, bacteria, and viruses accidentally attacks the myelin sheath—a protective coating over the nerve fibers called the axons—in the central nervous system. The central nervous system include a person's brain, optic nerves, and spinal cord (National Institute of Neurological Disorders and Stroke, 2020).

MS affects people differently. The white matter which are axons in the central nervous system guarded by myelin is attacked by MS. MS damages the nerve cell bodies in the brain's gray matter, axons in the brain, spinal cord, and optic nerves that pass on visual information from the eye to the brain. The outermost layer of the brain, called the cerebral cortex, shrinks when the disease is progressing; this is known as cortical atrophy. MS is known for the distinctive areas of scar tissue called plaques or lesions that occur from the immune system attacking the myelin. Plagues can be different sizes (National Institute of Neurological Disorders and Stroke, 2020).

There are several types of multiple sclerosis with various symptoms associated with the disease. MS symptoms can range from eye and vision issues, bladder problems, tingling, numbness, or pain, in arms, legs, torso, or face; weakness and spasticity in the muscles, painful muscle spasms, gait disturbance, fatigue, depression, and cognitive dysfunction and emotional changes (National Institute of Neurological Disorders and Stroke, 2020). Other symptoms of MS can include itching, dysesthesia, tremor, seizures, vertigo, dizziness, hearing loss, swallowing difficulties, loss of taste, sexual issues, depression, and breathing issues (MS Signs & Symptoms, n.d.). A small amount of people with MS will have a mild course with some to no disability while other MS symptoms may worsen leading to disability over time. However, a majority of people living with MS experience short periods of symptoms followed by long inactivity or dormancy with partial or full recovery (National Institute of Neurological Disorders and Stroke, 2020).

People living with MS will have a normal life expectancy—the disease is rarely deadly. Women are more affected by MS than men. New treatments can decrease long-term disability for people living with MS. Currently, there is no cure for MS or ways to keep someone from developing MS. But research is being conducted daily to find the cause of MS and a cure (National Institute of Neurological Disorders and Stroke, 2020).

MS is the most common disabling neurological disease among young adults with the onset of symptoms occurring between the ages of twenty to forty years old (National Institute of Neurological Disorders and Stroke, 2020). When an MS exacerbation (known as a relapse or flare-up) occurs, a majority of the myelin, and to a lesser degree the axons, in the affected area are damaged or destroyed by different types of immune cells. This is called inflammation. The severity of the inflammation and the location of an area of the plagues mainly show in the brain stem, cerebellum, spinal cord, optic nerves, and the white matter surrounding the brain ventricles, which causes MS symptoms (National Institute of Neurological Disorders and Stroke, 2020).

The onset and duration of MS symptoms depends on the certain type of MS. MS symptoms may start a few days and go away quickly or develop more gradually over many years (National Institute of Neurological Disorders and Stroke, 2020). There are several types of MS, such relapsing-remitting multiple sclerosis, secondary-progressive multiple sclerosis, primary-progressive multiple sclerosis, and progressive-relapsing multiple sclerosis. Research is being conducted daily to understand more about the disease (National Institute of Neurological Disorders and Stroke, 2020).

There are some rare variants of MS such as Marburg variant MS and Balo's concentric sclerosis (National Institute of Neurological Disorders and Stroke, 2020). Marburg variant MS also known as malignant MS causes quick and persistent symptoms and decline in function that causes significant disability or even death soon after onset. Balo's concentric sclerosis is a variant that progresses quickly. The MRI can detect the concentric rings of myelin destruction (National Institute of Neurological Disorders and Stroke, 2020).

3

The Confrontation

The hardest lessons I had to learn in life came from being diagnosed with a neurological disorder. At the age of twenty-five, most young adults focus on building financial stability, forming an intimate partner relationship, traveling, nurturing their passion, and living life to the fullest. After being diagnosed with multiple sclerosis, I felt my life crumble into small pieces of uncertainty, fear, sadness, and resentment. The life I once knew as a twenty-five-year-old healthy and educated young adult was over. In my mind, I imagined being jobless, isolated, partially paralyzed, and rejected by people.

I believed in God and had seen Him work miracles. However, I knew that it would take great faith to believe God would heal me from an incurable disease. In fact, in my mind, I thought I was in the clear of not developing any illness because I kept drugs and alcohol out of my body, and I stayed out of trouble. So, being diagnosed with an incurable disease was the last thing I thought would ever happen to me. I soon learned that being diagnosed with any illnesses or medical condition did not have an age, race, lifestyle, or gender requirement.

Entitlement

The first lesson I learned after my diagnosis was entitlement. Yes, I am a Christian, educated, and a friendly and caring person, but those things did not prevent me from being diagnosed with an illness. Weeks after my treatment, I repeated the exact phrase every day, "Why did this happen to me?" A broken record played every minute of my life until bitterness and resentment settled into my soul. I thought God was punishing me.

Finally, my mother came to me one day and said, "Sierra, why not you? Do you think these little children, teenagers, or adults and their families with cancer or other illnesses want to be sick? No, they do not! There are people with diseases who are in wheelchairs and walking on canes. You ought to be grateful. Not only that, but Jesus also had to go through being rejected and killed. Do you think His life was easy? Well, Sierra, news flash, it was not. So, Sierra, get yourself together because I'm not having a pity party with you."

I could not think of an explanation quick enough to rebut my mother's statement because deep down inside my heart, I knew she was right. However, my selfishness and pride made me blind to thinking about anyone but myself.

So, I told my mother, "I'm not talking about them right now. I want to know why this happened to me. Why couldn't I have a normal life without being sick? I'm ready to live my life now!"

My mother looked me in the eyes and walked away with disappointment. I felt like a fool and was left to reflect and ponder on my irrational thinking. I realized then that my multiple sclerosis journey would be a battle I had to fight mentally and physically.

I experienced pain in my body every day. Sometimes the pain seemed unbearable. I would experience muscles spasms in my legs, arms, and hands. I had terrible MS hugs, known as dysesthesia in medical terms. The MS hugs felt like having a heart attack, and a tight band was around my chest until I felt like I could not breathe sometimes. My feet had neuropathy; it felt like I was walking on a coal fire. I would experience headaches so bad that my mother would warm towels in the dryer and wrapped them around my head. I noticed that my headaches were severe, and I had pressure behind my eyes that was unbearable, so I scheduled an appointment with the ophthalmologist.

Dr. Hillard found that my optic nerve had inflammation, a medical condition called optic neuritis, and he became concerned about my vision. A visual field test came out normal. Dr. Hillard put me on acetazolamide, a medication that would assist me with releasing the fluid on my optic nerve and reduce the inflammation. He encouraged me to start a healthy meal plan and lose weight to reduce the swelling on my optic nerve.

I always wonder why my mother remained firm in her belief that she would not feel sorry for me and have pity parties with me. My mother is a great woman of strength and faith. A particular story came to mind when my mother went in for a routine mammography to start breast cancer screening once a year. The scan showed unusual spots on her breast. The examiners believed the areas were possibly cancer. She did not immediately return to receive another mammography as directed by the doctor, but instead went home and faithfully prayed for weeks for God to give her direction.

Finally, mom stated that God told her she would be alright. She then went back to the breast center to receive additional imaging. The follow-up mammography came back, and the doctor called her and said, "Mrs. Hairston, we are not sure what occurred, but your mammogram showed no spots." The doctor asked my mother to come in again for another mammography. The results still showed no marks on her breast. The doctor was amazed and ruled out breast cancer. The doctor encouraged my mother to continue to attend annual mammography for her breasts, and every year she would follow the doctor's order.

Pity Party with Cake and Balloons

I spent most days lying in bed and wondering how my life changed in the blink of an eye. I cried all the time and questioned God about His purpose in giving me a test that I was not strong enough to handle. I went through a grieving phase. I thought I would never become the successful and influential person I worked so hard to build in college. Throughout grade school and college, I struggled with my self-esteem and self-confidence. To be honest, as a child, I was diagnosed with attention-deficit/hyperactivity disorder. I struggled with paying attention, organization, staying on task, hyperactivity, and impulsiveness.

Over the years, I had to pray to God to give me the attentiveness and self-control to be successful in school. I did not feel good or smart enough. It took me longer to complete tests and stay on task, but I learned to go at my own pace and focus enough. My mother brought me crossword puzzles, newspaper comic strips, and math booklets to train my mind to focus and sharpen my skills. I enjoyed solving crossword puzzles and reading newspaper comic strips; however, math problems were challenging. I worked hard to study to become what I felt an extraordinary student represented: focused, driven, and motivated.

My achievements in school, especially in college, validated me as a person and was my driving force to strive for excellence. So, the fact that I could not hide my insecurities behind an award or people's verbal validation and praise hurt me deeply. I was forced to deal with myself as a bitter and insecure young lady. I was not regularly attending church at the time and had not in a while. Instead, I watched services online and visited other churches. I found it challenging to communicate with people, and I had times when I would not engage with my family. I closed my blinds and stayed in my bed for days, neglecting my emotional and physical health.

My mother eventually became frustrated with my no-care attitude and behavior. When my mother would go to work in the evening, and I was having a terrible night or MS symptoms, I called my mother to complain about my symptoms and express my dislike for what God did to me. My mother stopped taking calls from me and would not check on me at night. She told me that I needed to go to God in prayer to repent for the awful things I let come out of my mouth and start speaking life, blessings, and healing over my body. She encouraged me to pray, listen to a sermon, and read the Bible. My mother found some healing scriptures that she encouraged me to start reciting every day and wear on my body to remind me that God is a healer. Of course, I did not listen, and I remained stubborn and angry. My mother came into my room one afternoon and told me to get myself together, and she would not feel sorry for me because my situation could always be worse.

One Sunday, my mother turned on the television to watch a sermon by Dr. Charles Stanley. The teaching lasted for several weeks. I found out it was a series called, "In the School of Faith." My mother turned on the television in the living room every Sunday at 11:00 am so she could listen.

I grappled with the negative inner-chatter with the utmost resentment in my heart. My mother told me that the sermon was good and would help me with my faith. I refused to go into the living room and listen to anything about God or religion. Since I did not get the life I wanted, I told myself that I would not pray or serve God. I thought it would make me feel better, and if I rejected God, it would prompt Him to change my life because He would miss out on a good servant. However, as the days passed, my MS symptoms got worse. My headaches became unbearable, my muscle spasms out of control, and my overall body felt weaker. I knew God was trying to get my attention.

In denial, and trying to bargain with God, I railed against the changes MS would bring. I remained firm, believing that I would not tell anyone about my diagnosis and this disease would pass. My mother and older sister understood the importance of telling people about my diagnosis when I was ready. Unfortunately, my father decided to share my diagnosis with some family members when I did not want to share, so anyone can imagine a lot of talking and questioning occurred. I became upset and mad for a while because I believe people have a right to share their diagnoses in their own time. My mother's encouragement to move forward and share my diagnosis with my friends and people remained strong. She believed if I shared my diagnosis earlier, I would find and connect with other young people who have MS. Still, my heart was closed off to letting people know about my diagnosis.

I thought long and hard about what my mother said, and days later, I decided to tell a friend about my diagnosis. I remember feeling afraid to tell her, but I gained the courage to share. I started to cry, and I told her about the MRI scan finding three legions on my brain, and the side effects I experienced. She remained silent for a few minutes and then informed me that she thought it might have been something like MS because of my symptoms. I frequently communicated with her, and I told her about my symptoms. She remained calm and decided to pray with me over the phone. I felt supported and happy. She also told me that another young adult we knew mutually had MS. I contacted her several weeks later because I needed to speak with someone else like me. We had lunch one day and talked about our symptoms and living with MS. I felt empowered and encouraged with our meeting and excited to know another young adult African American woman living with MS. I felt like I was not alone.

My Heart is Open to a New Beginning

One Sunday, I decided to join my mother in the living room and listen to Dr. Charles Stanley's teaching series. This sermon was titled "Wavering Faith." I did not tell anyone, but I sought to change my attitude and my heart. My mother said that a voice came to her and said I needed to listen to the sermon because it would change my life. I decided to get out of my bed, sit on the sofa, and open my heart and ears to listen to God's teachings.

The sermon touched my heart at that moment. I discovered that to live a life pleasing to God, I must have unwavering faith that does not come and go. I must believe in God and take Him at His word. Memories flooded my mind on how God allowed me to complete my schooling while facing difficult obstacles. I started to feel guilty and unsure if God would forgive me for turning my back on Him. But I decided to take a chance and pray daily. I even started to read the Bible. I found that God's love for me never changed, and His heart remained pure. I began to spend a lot of time thinking and talking to God after the series.

My mother started to take me outside to sit under the oak tree in the backyard. We talked about life and what I expected in my MS journey. We prayed and believed that things would get better. I enjoyed those times. When I felt overwhelmed, my mother encouraged me to go outside under the oak tree to talk. We had heart-to-heart conversations and laughed. She encouraged me to start journaling to express my thoughts and start my healing process. She also encouraged me to start dancing again because she knew dancing was my passion and felt dancing would be a way to combat and improve my MS symptoms. My mother told me my healing was in my dancing. Being outside under the oak tree was a safe place for me to express my worries, cry, pray, meditate, read healing scriptures and the Bible, and have some serenity in my life. One night, I was experiencing a bad headache, and my mother prayed over me fervently. Then, all of a sudden, I felt a jolt of electricity go through my head. My mom felt some static going through her hand while praying. Since that night, my headaches decreased.

Often, most days I would look out the window of my bedroom to gaze at the beautiful sunsets. Sunsets were one of my favorite elements of nature because it is the most natural, vivid, and unfiltered paint canvases in the world. On the days when my body was weak and in pain, I looked forward to seeing the sunset outside my window because it reminded me that every day is not the same but carries beauty in it. The hues of blue, pink, yellow, and fresh orange from the sunset warmed my heart with joy.

On the days that I felt good, I would often journal under the oak tree in the evening. There was no distraction from my cell phone, people, or television when journaling outdoors. I had a quiet space full of country wildlife, sounds of birds, cows, dogs, hunters hunting, trees blowing in the wind, and traffic passing. One day, I heard a gentle voice from heaven above tell me to look out the window, and that is when I saw the most beautiful and colorful sunset right outside my home. I took a photo and journaled what I felt in my heart. I called the journal entry, "As

You Live Remember." I knew that one day I would use that sunset photo and inspirational message to share with the world.

My mother noticed that I spent more time reading the Bible and less time complaining about my life. I began to listen to different sermons by Dr. Charles Stanley. I found joy while journaling; it was like someone turned on a light switch, and the dark room became light. Journaling became a way that I could process my thoughts and be transparent about my feelings. My journal writings had the MS symptoms I was experiencing, gratitude notes, and prayers to improve my health. Through the process of journaling, my mother and I discovered my gift for writing inspirational messages. I prayed that the words would reach people living everyday life dealing with challenging situations. I hoped the writings would help people feel uplifted, inspired, empowered, and motivated.

I started to listen to gospel music from various artists and groups and danced throughout the day even when I felt weak. My mother always told me that she believed that my healing came from dancing and trusting in God. I felt happy while dancing, even for a few seconds or minutes. Dancing took away my fears, and I felt free. I did not feel as much pain in my body when I danced. I began to realize that my MS diagnosis was something that could not be forgotten and pushed aside.

Growing up in the south, we have an old saying, "Prayer works." I'm a witness to that statement. The more I prayed, the better my days seem to be, and the more God revealed the things that were in my heart. In prayer, God began to show me that I had unforgiveness towards several people. I started to pray for my enemies, the people I mistreated, and the people that mistreated me. Every moment I prayed, I felt stronger in my mind and body. The burden of unforgiveness got lighter every day.

I started to attend church more often. I visited my church with my sister one Sunday in early June 2016, and the spirit of God moved heavily in the service. For about twenty minutes, prayers and praises were given to God by the congregation. I decided to start giving thanks and honor to God. I began to feel my mouth drop and my tongue curl in my mouth, and I began to speak in tongues for the first time. In the Christian faith, speaking in tongues is evidence that you have received the Holy Spirit, which I like to call the voice. My heart filled with joy, and I knew that I needed to revisit some people from my past, forgive them, and ask them for forgiveness. I experienced a peace that day that I did not have for a while, and it felt great to be among the body of Christ again. For days, I spent time reading and meditating on the scriptures from the Bible. Two days later, I would have a vision that would forever set the tone for my multiple sclerosis journey.

The Healing Place Vision

The morning that changed my life forever happened on Tuesday, June 7, 2016. I had been taking painful injections for months, but this one was the most painful because the needle was sharp and pierced my skin enough to bleed lightly. My mother, as usual, gave me the injection in the evening before she left for work. My heart was heavy because I wondered if I would have to receive those painful injections for the rest of my life and if I would have the opportunity to live a life with purpose. I woke up with flu-like symptoms, fever, chills, and body aches. Tears streamed down my cheeks, and I asked God, "God, I need to know if you are going to heal me, and if not, how do you want me to live my life?"

I went back to sleep, but several hours later, a voice woke me up. The presence was powerful but calm. It told me, "Sierra, I would like to take you to a place."

I was thinking to myself, no, I'm not ready to die. I still have more life to live. I'm not prepared to leave this earth.

The voice pleaded with me a few more times and finally told me, "Sierra, I think that you will like this place. You will live."

I decided to surrender my will and mind, and I started to fall slowly into a deep sleep, but I felt a strong presence pulling my body as if my soul was leaving my body. I was not in control of my body. I then saw complete darkness and heard a loud freight train, and the closer I got to this place, the train sound got louder.

Suddenly, the darkness of the tunnel I was traveling through became bright. My eyes awoke to sunny, fluffy clouds passing my face. Stunned at what I was witnessing, I said aloud, "Where am I?"

Then I saw an older adult man with a woman who appeared to be a nurse walking in scrubs. Next, I saw a middle-aged woman and child sitting on a concrete fountain. I focused on the mother and child because they were wearing the color white. They were coughing and holding their stomach and throats like they were in agonizing pain. Suddenly some pills appeared in the air. The child and woman took the medication and instantly started to feel better. They stretched and smiled and appeared to be grateful.

Puzzled by what I saw, my focus turned to the older man and who appeared to be his nurse. They both were wearing the color wine. The older man was walking with a walker, and his feet appeared to shuffle. He told his nurse that he could not wait until his surgery to walk again. The nurse told him once he gets his surgery, he would feel much better. They both smiled at each other and went along.

Then soon after, I heard thunder and saw tremendous legs coming from the cloud, which appeared to be walking directly behind the older man and nurse. The legs then stopped once it noticed that I was looking and bent down to look at me. I saw that a human-like giant figure was wearing a wine-colored robe. A bright light covered the face and hair. I covered my eyes because the light was so bright, and I was afraid. I trembled with fear. The human-like figure looked at me, moved along, and followed the older man and nurse. I realized at that moment that the human-like giant figure was the man's guardian angel sent to watch over him in surgery.

I then appeared in a place surrounded by clouds that revealed a beautiful water fountain that released crystal-clear water. A chair appeared in front of the fountain, and I heard a voice say sit down. I walked over to the fountain and sat down in the chair. Next, the voice instructed me to saturate my head and face with the water from the fountain, so I did. I even tasted the water that ran down my face, but the water was tasteless.

Finally, the gentle voice told me to stop washing my face, and I received my healing. Immediately, I stopped washing my face and walked away from the chair with gratitude. The voice then told me, "Sierra, before you go back, I want to let you know that whatever you do, never stop believing you are healed, no matter what."

I anxiously said "Okay," and the voice repeated the exact phrase twice. I woke up from the vision in my bed at three o'clock in the morning, in awe and amazement.

Purpose of the Vision

Weeks before my vision, I meditated and often prayed about my healing. I spoke Bible scriptures and positive affirmations over my life. I often wondered why God chose to heal some people while other people passed away. My mother always told me that whether God chooses to heal someone on this earth or take them, it is still a win; nobody has lost the battle to an illness they have won. They are winners. As I reflected on my vision, diseases affected people of different ages and stages of life, and conditions can be stabilized or healed through medication, surgery, and in my case, supernaturally. I also noticed the specific colors white, and wine were in the vision. The biblical color of wine represented new birth, multiply, and overflow (Olesen, n.d.). The biblical color for white represented Bride of Christ, joy, peace, righteousness, blessedness, light, angels, saints, harvest, surrender, conquest, triumph, completion, and victory (Olesen, n.d.). I felt like God answered my prayers. However, His promise was conditional under the terms that I believe in my healing no matter the situation. After the vision, my life would take a turn for the worse.

4

The Fight

A few weeks after my healing vision, my physical health turned for the worse. The strength in my physical body weakened. I could not walk without getting spasms in my legs, back, and hands. My legs were so wobbly and stiff it was as if I was walking on Jell-O° and quicksand at the same time. My feet felt like they were walking on hot coals. My hands became like claws due to spasticity. Picking up a glass of water and opening my medication bottle became difficult. My acid reflux worsened.

Several weeks later, I woke up with my throat feeling like sandpaper. I decided to drink warm water with honey and gargled with warm salt water, but nothing helped. I started to have difficulty swallowing liquids and solid foods. I discussed my health concerns with my mother. She believed that my poor diet of chocolate candy bars, greasy food, and acidic drinks triggered my acid reflux symptoms. But I felt this time something different was going on with my throat besides the acid reflux. I woke up days later with a severely dry mouth, and I could not swallow saliva or drink water without choking.

My mother and I called the gastroenterologist. Fortunately, a follow-up upper endoscopy already scheduled was moved up to an emergency procedure. I entered the gastroenterology center weak, thirsty, and scared. My pulse rate got as high as 124. My gastroenterologist performed the procedure and determined that I had dysphagia, a swallowing disorder that affects someone's ability to swallow adequately. After the exam, my gastroenterologist gave me two bags of saline intravenous drip because I was so dehydrated. There was nothing she could give me for relief because the condition was an underlying condition of MS. She told me to gargle with salt water, be careful with drinking liquids, and eat soft foods until the situation eased. We spoke with the healthcare team, and the option of a feeding tube came up if I could not receive the nutrients I needed through eating soft food and drinking liquids. For weeks, I drank nutritional shakes and water. I ate peach fruit cups, saltine crackers, mashed potatoes, and soft bread.

A Birthday to Remember

My birthday was a day to reflect. It was a day like no other. I turned twenty-six years old on July 31, 2016, three months after being diagnosed with MS. I still had difficulty swallowing and was on a liquid and soft food diet. I asked my mother to fix her delicious homemade moist pineapple cake for my birthday, and she agreed. I did not have the energy to go anywhere, and I struggled eating soft and solid food, so there was no need to go for a birthday lunch or dinner.

I went through a series of emotions. I felt a sense of joy and gratitude for making it to see my birthday, but I was also overwhelmed with sadness, bitterness, and resentment. I still wanted to be a healthy young adult who was independent and living my best life, free of health issues. I did not wish to be sick and resented that I had to live a life with illness and uncertainty. Discouraged, I put on a brave face and smiled, but deep down, I felt afraid and alone. My symptoms appeared to worsen daily. My mother and sister tried their best to brighten my day by speaking positive things and giving me birthday gifts that they knew I would like. They sang the happy birthday song, and I cut my cake; however, I attempted to swallow a small piece of pineapple cake and felt like the cake lodged in my throat. I gagged and choked on my cake. I thought to myself, *Wow, this is how it ends, huh?*

My mother immediately asked me to pray over my body and read the healing scriptures she gave me. I had a folded piece of paper with healing scriptures tucked in my bra to hold close to my body to remind me of God's words of healing.

My mother and sister joined in my prayer, and we started to pray over my throat, and I begin to feel a little better. After my cake eating failed, I read my birthday greeting cards and opened my presents while sitting on my bed. The heartfelt words of the cards and the gifts lifted my spirits. I started to cry because I understood that I was loved, supported, and valued by my family. My sadness turned to joy, and I enjoyed my birthday. I rested the remainder of the day and medicated my body with acetaminophen to prepare my body to receive my treatment injection. Through the months of my emotional ups and downs after my MS diagnosis, my family practiced patience, self-control, and exhibited unconditional love.

What are You Hiding From?

My symptoms worsened as the week passed through August 2016. I continued to journal and dance through my days. I tried to go outside to walk Jack for about ten to fifteen minutes to get Jack some fresh air and, at the same time, improve my mental health. I experienced terrible allergy symptoms and I felt so congested that at times it was difficult to breathe. I took allergy medication to assist with my symptoms. I still hid my diagnosis from people and most times did not want to acknowledge the disease. The added stress of hiding my diagnosis and body in a full MS exacerbation or flare up made my MS ongoing and non-stop. I felt compelled to continue to pray over my body and stay optimistic. I spoke with my neurologist, and he ordered me to begin outpatient rehab to strengthen my gait, weakness, and coordination.

I believed the more I listened to sermons and prayed, the worse my symptoms got. My body became so weak that I lost my voice and ended up spending a few hours in the emergency room. On August 31, 2016, I arrived at the emergency room weak and with no voice. I received an examination and lab tests. The physician assistant informed me that, most likely, I had a viral infection that caused laryngitis. He stated that my immune system appeared to be impacted by my ongoing underlying conditions related to MS. I rested for a few days until I felt better. Luckily, my body symptoms improved. My MS relapse lasted for several months. I attended my first session in outpatient rehab on September 7, 2016.

I remember walking into outpatient rehab feeling afraid and guarded. I saw an African American woman who looked like she was in her mid-twenties. She appeared to have a drop foot, and she was walking on a cane. I also saw a middle-aged man with a prosthetic leg walking the treadmill and an older man carrying a Parkinson's notebook. I thought to myself, *What world did I just enter?*

Then, I met my physical therapist. She was a young adult female that was patient and compassionate. She helped me do strength exercises with my legs and assisted me with coordination and balance. I also completed neurological physical activities. The most challenging exercise for me to do was called a clamshell. The African American woman looked at me, smiled, and said the clamshell exercise is challenging but will give my legs a good workout. I smiled back at her, and I felt supported. I attended outpatient rehab for six weeks.

After attending outpatient rehab, I felt empowered to fight through the physical challenges brought to me by multiple sclerosis. My MS symptoms were ongoing, and my neurologist ordered an MRI in September to check for additional lesions because my symptoms appeared to progress. A few days later, I was wrestling with anxiety and fear, so I decided to do something bold. I needed to change the scenery of always being in the house, praying. I walked outside on the back porch and screamed out loud, "I'm not waiting to receive my healing. I am getting my healing now." I cried and declared, "God, you told me no matter what, I'm going to choose to believe."

I continued to read healing scriptures and speak positive affirmations over my life. I knew my MRI was coming up soon, and it was up to me to declare my healing in advance. I received direction from God to find stories in the Bible of people who exhibited extraordinary faith and perseverance. Some of the stories I read from the Bible were Daniel in the Lion's Den, David and Goliath, Job, the Samaritan woman at the well, a woman with the issue of blood, the blind beggar, and more stories. I meditated on the stories day and night, and I also continued to journal and dance.

Second MRI Results

On September 28, 2016, I had my second MRI. I did not get as nervous as I did the first time. I knew what to expect. When I entered the mobile MRI scanner, peace came over me. I closed my eyes and reflected on the stories of faith I read, and God began to speak to me and said, "Share your testimony and focus on a ministry about rejection, love, forgiveness, and hope."

In that moment, I had a better idea of why the uninvited guest arrived, but at the time, it did not make it any easier. Days later, I received a call from my neurologist nurse. She informed me that I had no new lesions on my brain and my lesions appeared to decrease in size. My mother and I set up an appointment with the neurologist to discuss my MRI findings. On October 4, 2016, we met with my neurologist, Dr. Hansen. He informed us that my labs were good, and the MRI showed that the white matter on my brain decreased, and the three lesions on my brain shrunk significantly. The most extensive lesion located on the thalamus part of the brain initially looked like the size of a large grapefruit, but the new MRI showed my lesion was the size of a peanut. The two lemon-sized lesions located on the back of my brain shrunk to the size of a pinpoint dot.

Dr. Hansen looked at me and said, "Ms. Hairston, I don't know what occurred. I talked to my other colleagues in this profession and specialty, and we all had no explanation on how your brain lesions shrunk. I can't say for sure, but it's almost as if your brain healed itself."

He told me to continue to stay on treatment, exercise, and eat a healthy diet. I smiled and knew that God's promises of my healing stood true. My mother and I left the appointment thanking God for his healing power and feeling more optimistic regarding the remission phase of my MS. We considered me a modern-day miracle.

What is Next?

I spent the remainder of 2016 building my faith and focusing on little things out of life that brought me joy, like waking up in the morning, the ability to touch the dew on the grass in the morning, and walking with my dog Jack in the yard. I still had MS symptoms, but I had to believe what God told me. I thought it would take great faith to receive a profound and life-changing message from God. It turned out it only took having a conversation with God and preparing my heart to listen. I just wanted to live my life with purpose. My journaling increased, and I wrote passionate letters to God. I had a great desire to share my testimony about what God did, but I feared that I would be a poster child for MS, and people would treat me differently. At that time, I still valued what people thought about me. People's opinions were how I gained my self-esteem and self-worth. I thought my life would be limited if I recognized I had MS. Honestly, I still desired not to be ill. I wanted to explore the world and be recognized for my accomplishments, not living with a chronic illness. But the uninvited guest still had other plans.

5

Breakthrough

The year of 2017 arrived, and the uninvited guest, MS, never left my party. We fought a bitter battle for over seven months, but MS remained persistent in its plan not to go. I wondered what it would take for MS and myself to part ways. But isn't it funny how divine purpose is not easily defined or understood?

My treatments continued; I spent more time journaling and praying to God. I started to feel better physically. I discussed with my mother about working a job, but we both concluded that I might have to change the type of job to accommodate my health. I still had the desire to become a licensed clinical social worker. My mother continued to encourage me to study for my clinical exam and keep myself updated on the things occurring in the social work profession. I was disappointed because I felt like my physical health challenges and stubborn ways were why I could not get ahead in life.

I started to notice that every time I began to feel sorry for myself, God would allow me to see someone in a wheelchair or use a walking aid as a reminder that I needed to be grateful for the ability to walk despite my challenges. In prayer, God revealed the year 2017 would be the year for a breakthrough. The year to breakthrough barriers I set up to block people out of my life. The two main barriers were hiding my diagnosis and being too prideful to ask people for help.

The spring arrived, and I looked forward to taking my dog Jack for walks in the yard. I discovered my love of nature. Jack had grown accustomed to me getting his walking vest out of his dog bag, so when he heard me getting his vest out, he automatically jumped from his bed and ran to me so I could put his vest on. He enjoyed walking in the yard with me. I loved to feel the cool breeze on my face and hear birds chirping. My mind was clear and in complete serenity.

My balance and coordination improved, and I felt more confident walking in the backyard for longer than thirty minutes. My swallowing difficulties lessened every day. While walking, I noticed that my parents' apple trees and the surrounding trees, like the oaks and others, were blooming. Although I grew up in the country and learned as a child and teenager how to plant seeds and harvest vegetable and fruit gardens from my mother (she grew up as a sharecropper in eastern North Carolina in the 1960s), I never took the time to appreciate the simplicity and beauty of nature. I didn't notice the fruit blooms from the trees were so beautiful until I observed them closely while walking with Jack.

After taking Jack for a walk in early April, 2017, I went back outside and took my first nature photo of the apple tree. My love for nature grew that season. The more time I spent walking in the yard with Jack, the more I became aware of my surroundings. The environment became beautiful to me because it represented life. I spent my spring and summer under the oak tree meditating, praying, journaling, singing, and taking photos of nature literally in my backyard.

A Letter to My Dear Mother

I became fond of writing as it became a way to express myself. I wrote a letter to my mother in August, 2017, to thank her for stepping up as not only my mother but my caregiver. I had difficulty taking a step back and accepting help from anyone, even my mother. My mother had recently experienced a bad car accident, the death of her youngest brother, transitioned out of a nursing leadership position for another opportunity, and still had to take care of her family and me. So, I felt the best gift I could give her was to write her a letter to express my gratitude.

The Letter

August 4, 2017
Mom,
The strength that you have shown and continue to show amazes me every day. I'm so proud of your accomplishments working as a Clinical Unit Leader on a challenging floor. You made the floor a more organized, accountable, and better floor for both the workers and management staff. All the while taking care of an ill daughter who lost her ability to eat, walk, stand, concentrate, and complete simple self-care tasks. You continued to work through the death of your brother, your husband's health issues, and many challenges the

family faced. You also had the responsibility of taking care of our pet Jack and being there for your oldest daughter. Not to mention having your health issues; even working with broken ribs you sustained from a severe car accident, you continued to work.

To the woman who listened to the voice of God that led me to listen to Charles Stanley ministries, thank you. To the woman who showed me the importance of trusting in God with all my heart, the importance of finishing a task, who paid for my medications and medical expenses, and did not let me lay down and die, I send you my complete love and gratitude.

Love your daughter,
Sierra

I remember my mother reading the letter and being in awe and grateful for how I expressed my words. My mother told me, "Sierra, do you know you have a gift of writing? You wrote your words so elegantly. I knew that you were always a great public speaker, but you are a writer as well. Sierra, you need to continue journaling and writing messages to encourage people who deal with hardship and everyday life."

I felt proud of myself and felt like I accomplished a lot at that moment. My mother was proud of how far I had come. I bashfully told my mother, "I don't know Mom."

My mother, with confidence, told me, "Sierra, use your words to be a blessing to people."

Show Yourself to the World

On my twenty-seventh birthday, I went to the production of Five Guys Named Moe at the National Black Theater Festival held in Winston-Salem, North Carolina, with my mother and sister. I felt beautiful that day because it was the first time I did not wear a t-shirt, pants, and tennis shoes. The play went well, and my family and I had a great time seeing different vendors and fellowshipping with people in the community. My feet were sore by the end of the night, but I was so happy. I told myself that I would continue to take the steps I needed to start living my life again.

One of my other favorite memories that occurred a few months after the theater festival was when my family and I went to the State Fair in North Carolina on October 22, 2017. We did not go for the rides, but we went for the food. The smell of pork, fried funnel cakes, corn, and smoked turkey legs filled my soul with warmth and happiness. I did not have the healthiest diet. Even though I knew having a healthy balanced diet and regular exercise was vital to reducing my MS symptoms, I still wanted to have my cake and eat it too. The food smelled so delicious. I had to have it. I thought to myself, *Let us eat!* Boy, did we eat! My sister and I shared a smoked turkey leg, a fried snicker, a powdered sugar funnel cake, a red velvet powdered sugar funnel cake, vanilla ice cream, and three pieces of corn each. We drank water to wash down all the delicious food.

My sister and I ate until we dropped. My sister joked and said we needed someone to wheelbarrow us to the car. Luckily our mother did not eat as much as we did, so she drove us home.

The food choices were not the best, but I wanted to try as much food as possible, considering I had swallowing difficulties the previous year. I remember several months prior having anxiety going in public because I feared my legs would buckle and I would be unable to walk. I did not want to face the looks and stares from people. However, I stepped out on faith that day and did not let anything get in my way. I felt fantastic being among people again and knew I was changing for the best.

Third MRI

My third annual MRI exam came on October 25, 2017. I did not feel nervous about my third MRI, and I did not feel any discomfort while in the mobile MRI scanner. I had a feeling that I would be alright. Days later, my neurologist nurse informed me that there were no changes to the MRI and my MS was stable. I felt relieved and grateful. I thought to myself, another year to celebrate God's grace and healing power. The year continued to bring about good changes that allowed me to be more independent. I started to drive again and took more effort and pride in how I physically looked.

Stop Being Afraid

The year 2018 arrived and brought significant change. I started to feel more compelled to reveal my diagnosis and tell people my story. However, I did not know how to go about doing so. Also, my ten-year high school class reunion was coming up in the fall, and I wanted to be free of any baggage. I soon started to develop fear and deep regret of not having a job and depending on my mother to take care of me. I began to feel sorry for myself again and did not want to go out to places with my family as much. I compared myself to other people my age.

By the age of twenty-eight, I thought I would have a solid career, buy my first house, and date an intelligent and respectful young man of God. But the fairytale story I wrote in my mind was not reality. I decided it would be best for me to start praying to God for direction. I felt like I needed to tell my story to set myself free, but I still had a conflict with myself and God. I knew it was time to tell more people because hiding my diagnosis burdened my soul, but I was not ready.

My mother came to me one day in March of 2018 and told me to get out of my funk. I believe my mother could tell I was feeling down because I did not have a job. She encouraged me to start using my God-given gifts, talents, abilities, social work skills, and transferrable skills to start a business and work for myself. My mother informed me about business classes held at our alma mater GTCC and another local community college called Alamance Community College (ACC). After weeks of my mother encouraging me to take business classes, I decided to put my pride aside and started taking courses in April of 2018. My mother attended business classes with me on the days she did not have to work.

I quickly realized that I needed to take time to learn about my purpose and start a business. Within weeks of attending business classes, I became an entrepreneur and businesswoman right before my mother's eyes. I have always been intelligent and ambitious. For the first time in a while, I felt like I could finally use my social work and transferrable skills to my advantage, considering I had been out of work for a few years. I was resourceful, computer literate, and tech-savvy. My mother was intelligent, business-minded, good with resources and finances, and had her Master's in Business Administration, so she knew how to prepare for a business. She had to work her full-time job as a registered nurse, so she let me catch her up on what we needed to do to start a business.

I dragged my feet initially until I encountered a nice woman God sent my way. I met her in Walmart. She greeted me while we were both on our way to the bathroom. She asked me how I was doing, and I pleasantly responded, good. We both used the bathroom and washed our hands. As we washed our hands at the bathroom sinks, she began a conversation about her recent retirement from a local healthcare system. I felt a strong pull from God to talk to this woman, so I continued to listen to the woman's story. Suddenly, she started to witness to me about starting a business, and she told me God wanted to know why I had not started the company yet.

I gave every excuse in the world, but she told me that God wanted me to use my social work skills and what I know to start a business to help people and not worry about the money needed for start-up. The situation shocked the woman and me. The woman informed me that God sometimes lays on her heart to speak to people, and she gets nervous approaching someone because she does not know their reaction. She told me that her being obedient to God is more important to her than someone's reaction. She stated that she was often amazed that God used her to speak to His people to bring a word of encouragement or confirmation. The woman and I gave thanks to God.

I believe the woman came as a form of confirmation because God had been telling me for weeks to start the business, but it did not make any sense to me because I had no money to contribute, so I declined. It is incredible how God can get your attention. I told my mother about the encounter, and she was not surprised because she told me to start the business and not worry about money. After deep thought and prayer, I decided to put things into motion, move forward, and start the business. However, the uninvited guest still had other plans.

Starting a New MS Treatment

My MS treatment was doing well for over a year, but several routine labs revealed that my white blood cell count consistently reported low. When the white blood count cell is down, it can compromise an individual's, immune system causing infections and other serious medical issues. My neurologist, Dr. Hansen, became concerned and reached out to me in the early spring of 2018. He called me and told me he thought it would be best to change my treatment. My mother and I became concerned and hesitant. We feared that the medication might bring on more symptoms, and we did not know how my body would react to changing treatment.

Dr. Hansen called several days later to hear my decision. We received patient education from him regarding new treatment and decided to try a new medicine in spring 2018, a one-a-day pill. The side effects of the medication were headaches and diarrhea. However, I believe the combination of a poor diet consisting of foods high in carbohydrates, fats, sugars, sodium, and not having a gallbladder contributed to my gastrointestinal distress. My mother always encouraged me to eat certain foods in moderation, exercise regularly, eat more fruits and vegetables, and drink plenty of water. But I did not listen and had to learn the hard way.

Unfortunately, I experienced several incidents in public when I did not have control over my bowels because I could not get to a toilet in enough time. Well, you know what happened next. I had to go home, change undergarments, and bathe myself. Those moments were painfully embarrassing, and I knew I needed to do a better job with my diet. Nonetheless, my family and I were pleased that I did not experience any significant side effects. My MS symptoms were still stable, and I did not relapse.

I started to put more emphasis on exercising and taking care of my health. I began to increase my daily exercise and eat healthy balanced meals. I walked at least thirty minutes a day and worked out with dumbbells. I began to feel like my body had more energy because I exercised. I knew I was supposed to exercise and have a healthier diet anyway, but the class reunion was a good incentive. I could tell my overall health was improving, and I started to lose weight. My eye health improved, and my ophthalmologist, Dr. Hillard, recommended that I stop taking acetazolamide because my optic nerve inflammation decreased significantly. He also suggested that I continue to exercise daily and maintain a healthy diet so the build-up of pressure on my optic nerve would not occur again.

Back to Business Part One

My mother and I worked diligently to choose our business category. We decided to start a greeting card business to inspire, encourage, enlighten, enhance, empower, and enrich people living everyday life. We also wanted to combine my mother's experience in the nursing field and my experience in the social work field to build a business based on service. We both loved to serve and give back to the community.

We came up with the unique business name, Timely Fountain. My mother believed that everything in life is released at the right time, and she came up with the word Timely. The word fountain was dear to my heart and a homage to my healing vision. I believed a fountain represented happiness, peace, healing, and serenity in life situations. We both thought that every fountain in life is released on time, giving people a higher purpose to keep living. Our slogan for our business is, "Enjoy Life and Breathe." Both our business name and slogan fit perfectly for our purpose and mission for the company.

After two failed attempts to receive a logo from two different freelance graphic designers, my mother encouraged me to create a logo for the business. I researched and taught myself how to create a logo for our business with a computer program. The logo I made turned out to be unique and symbolic. I also learned how to use the design tool from a computer software program to design a star for one of our greeting cards. We started to research greeting card categories and styles and spent days writing the card messages. We began to seek out freelance graphic designers to help design our cards and a print company to print our cards. We both were driven and motivated to invest in ourselves and the business. We did our research and taught ourselves how to submit our writings to the United States Copyright Office to protect our greeting card writings. We further did our research and decided to apply for a trademark with the United States Patent and Trademark Office to protect our business name and logo in August 2018.

I felt terrific and ready to embark on a new journey. However, a black cloud of heaviness followed me everywhere I went. I remember God telling me one day as I was fighting self-doubt, "Sierra, if you are not for yourself, who will be for you? If you are not rooting for yourself and being your cheerleader, no one will."

I eventually embedded that phrase in my heart and used it as a battle weapon to combat my fear and self-doubt. I prayed for God to allow me to tell a vast amount of people about my diagnosis. Days later, I saw an online post from a family member of an event being hosted at a local event center. I decided to call my family member to inform him of my interest in performing a liturgical dance routine, and he gladly added me to the program. I jumped at the opportunity because I had not danced in front of a crowd for several years.

I kicked things into gear and started choreographing my liturgical dance to the song *"I Worship You with All of Me"* by Mary Alessi. The day of the event arrived on August 18, 2018, and I will never forget it. I was excited and full of gratitude. I invited immediate family members, a friend, and one of my former dance teachers to the event.

I practiced backstage, and my mother and sister assisted me with getting ready. They then took their seats. My dad was already sitting in the audience. I felt a strong presence that I needed to tell my testimony, but I needed a sign. Then I was told by the event backstage helper that I could introduce myself or share a testimony before or after my dance if I wanted to. At that moment, I was utterly shocked but knew it was my opportunity to share my story. I told the backstage helper that I would share my testimony after I danced.

I entered the stage with grace and calmness. I knew my sister was recording my dance. As soon as the music started, I felt empowered and danced gracefully across the floor with my legs and dance flags. It was a magical moment, the song ended, and the crowd cheered. I walked off stage to collect my thoughts, and moments later, I walked back on stage and shared my testimony on how I was diagnosed with multiple sclerosis and the miracle that occurred with the lesions on my brain. Everyone was in awe of God's incredible power and grace. I knew in my heart that my mission to share my testimony of God's truth and power had just begun.

That day changed my trajectory on how I would tell people about my diagnosis. I researched and taught myself how to cut and arrange videos using a computer video editor program. I was proud of myself for cutting and editing my dance video. Nevertheless, I had difficulty releasing my dance testimony video on social media because my value was still in what people thought about me. The encouragement and motivation from my mother and sister inspired me to finally upload my video to an online video sharing and social media website in September of 2018.

Once I shared my video on my social media sites, I felt an enormous burden lifted off my shoulders. I received positive feedback and well wishes on my social media accounts from some people I knew from school, friends, family members, and associates. From that day forward, I decided that I would tell the world about my MS diagnosis to be a blessing to others living with multiple sclerosis or dealing with challenges and hardships.

High School Class Reunion

The day of my ten-year class reunion arrived in October of 2018. It would be the day to connect with people I have not seen in years. I arrived at the football game with my sister. I noticed that the football stadium looked the same. Memories from middle school and high school flooded my mind. I thought it was a blessing from God to have the opportunity to come back to my class reunion and be in good health. It showed how resilient I was in the face of adversity. I saw a few classmates at the game and greeted them. They were glad to see me and told me that I looked good, and they were delighted to know that I was doing well.

I had the opportunity to greet and hug so many of my classmates. I also saw a few of my high school crushes and chuckled to myself. In the evening, I blossomed and flourished into a social butterfly. I had good conversations with my classmates and took photos with them and my sister. I informed one classmate about my medical condition, and he was so shocked that his mouth opened wide as he stared intently. I smiled and gracefully walked away. I did not let anything hold me back. Some classmates I was friends with on social media at the class reunion told me my dance testimony video touched their hearts. I felt wonderful sharing my testimony. Overall, my experience was better than I thought, and I left the reunion feeling content.

Fourth MRI

My fourth annual MRI happened on November 7, 2018. I did not fret or become fearful because I knew that my results would turn out well. I listened to a sermon by Dr. Charles Stanley to prepare for the MRI. I had no pain or discomfort while taking the scan. Days later, my neurologist nurse informed me that there were no changes to the MRI and my MS was stable. My response to myself was, *God, did it again!*

Back to Business Part Two

In mid-November, 2018, my mother and I attended our first vending event for our greeting cards. We took photos with our customers, and we looked forward to attending other vending events in the community to showcase our greeting cards. As I reflected on my year, I realized that I accomplished several goals such as stepping outside of my shell, revealing my MS diagnosis and shortcomings to people, discovering my God-given gifts and talents, starting a business, and receiving an excellent health report. I learned that confronting and facing uncomfortable situations presented an opportunity for growth and maturity.

6

Reconciliation

I felt compelled to start interacting with the multiple sclerosis community. My mother always encouraged me to reach out to the MS community and share my story because other young people like me had similar experiences. But, for over two years, I decided not to engage with the community because I did not want to get treated differently. I was also secretly scared to put myself out in the open because I struggled with my confidence, self-value, and self-worth for years. When MS came into my life, it further strained my self-esteem. I was barely hanging on by a thread.

My mother always taught me to have high self-esteem and value myself. Still, I struggled because I wanted to be accepted by everyone and had difficulty putting myself out front because I worried about what people thought about me. I did not want to get unwanted attention and face the judgment of people. I did not fully embrace my unique abilities, gifts, and talents. But I realized that I could not hide behind a closed door forever because MS was too big of a thing not to be acknowledged.

My mother always found stories of people living with MS from magazines in my neurology center or the internet to inspire me, but she wanted me to connect with the community directly. She encouraged me to reach out to the MS community to be inspired and empowered. I started to look up MS-related content on the internet and social media. I heard about the National Multiple Sclerosis Society from my neurologist and healthcare team, but did not take the time to investigate what the organization offered. In my search, I learned that the National Multiple Sclerosis Society (National MS Society) was a nonprofit organization connecting people, community partners, organizations, and the MS community. The National MS Society brought awareness, advocacy, education, research, programs, and services specifically for people with multiple sclerosis.

Test the Waters

I started to engage in the MS community and continued participating in community service with my mother and sister. I focused more on being an advocate in the MS community, volunteering, attending events with my family and friends, and investing in my greeting card business with my mother. I started to release MS from the chokehold that I had it in for over a year. I had to catch my breath and regain my strength. I wrestled and fought a hard battle with MS. I felt the chains of stress and burden lift off me.

I remember a unique customer interaction that brightened my day during a Mother's Day Vending Event, making all the pain and suffering I dealt with worthwhile. A middle-aged woman walked past our table and commented that she liked our Mother's Day Cards and T-shirts. The shirt had our business slogan, "Enjoy Life and Breathe," displayed on it. She bought two shirts and a greeting card. She told me the phrase was encouraging because she was recently diagnosed with liver cancer and would start treatment soon. I told her about my MS diagnosis and some of the obstacles I faced. She and I both encouraged and hugged one another.

My sister helped me with vending at a flea market, and I met a middle-aged woman who liked our "Enjoy Life and Breathe" T-shirts. She shared with us that her husband went through a battle with lung cancer, and she always told him to breathe, and he would breathe. Unfortunately, he passed away. She told us that she struggled to move on and wanted to know if it was okay to move on. She believed that God sent her a confirmation through our company slogan because the shirt stated "Enjoy Life and Breathe." She believed God and her husband were telling her to move on and enjoy life. She gladly purchased the T-shirt. I felt like crying because I thought about how everything worked together perfectly when God is in the midst of any situation. I knew that my pain and suffering had a purpose, just like God told me.

An Opportunity for Growth

You know the saying: Momma always knows best. Well she did. She saw greater for me than just working a job and wanted me to explore all my options. I believed God gave me the free will to choose my job but encouraged me to focus on nurturing my God-given gifts, ability, talents, and business, and not concentrate on obtaining a position to make money.

College Homecoming

I decided to attend my college homecoming with my family in late October of 2019. NC A&T SU homecoming had the best events, performances, and vendors, and embraced the community with open arms. NC A&T SU homecoming is known as the Greatest Homecoming on Earth (GHOE). I felt appreciative coming back to campus, considering all the battles I fought. One of the events I attended was a social work department event. I fellowshipped with my former classmates, current students, and professors. My professors were so proud of my progress and saw my growth and maturity. I also had the opportunity to share my testimony of living with MS and gave words of encouragement to current students in the undergraduate social work program regarding life and choosing a career during a break-out session with current and former students. I felt proud of myself and ready to continue living my life.

It Takes Faith

As I reflect on 2019, it was the year that I completely stepped outside of my comfort zone. I took chances on myself, increased the visibility and sales of my greeting cards business, reached out to the MS community, completed a job training program, earned a certification, received an excellent MRI report, and obtained employment. Most importantly, I built a stronger relationship and trust with God. My purpose became more remarkable, and I knew that with anything that happened in the future, I would be able to draw my hope and strength from the storms, trials, sets backs, and victories that I experienced, and I would make it.

To the Uninvited Guest, Thank You for Coming

The guest that arrived at my door gave me an unexpected gift that I could not forget or push aside. I received the gift of resilience and perseverance. To my surprise, the gift brought wholeness and purpose that I could not obtain had it not come unexpectedly in my life. Sometimes when we find our lives difficult, we can resent our lives and blame others for our life difficulties. My tale of self-defeat and long-suffering gave me the ability to discover my true self—a compassionate, caring, hardworking, and creative soul. I learned that my life experiences were not only for myself but to encourage and empower others.

We think it takes perfection to be an example for God, but I have learned that it takes surrendering all thoughts and actions to God for Him to direct your path. No one will ever be perfect, and most times, our perfection will never meet our expectations, so, it's easier just being your flawed and authentic self and allowing God to lead the way. Most importantly, what you think about yourself or how you value yourself will set you on a path to success or failure.

In closing, I will leave you with some words of encouragement. May you know that your worth and value are not determined by your accomplishments or even life's obstacles, but by your perseverance and never giving up on yourself. Please share your story of setbacks, failures, triumphs, and victories with people because we are here to serve, uplift, and empower one another. Life is not without challenges, so breathing in trials (accepting those challenges) and breathing out strength (exhibiting perseverance) will keep you growing and learning to enjoy life and live.

Don't be afraid to ask for help. When good people come into your life as a caregiver, family, friend, medical professional team, or another critical role, be transparent about how you feel and what is happening in your life. Cherish them and know that they are there to help you and want the best for you. I hope that you will live a life of opportunities to reflect, learn, grow, and stand tall on your foundation so you can be a ray of light in someone's life.

Sometimes uninvited guests arrive in your life at an unexpected time that may inconvenience your plans. So, learn to take the good things with the bad things and keep thriving through life. There is always a lesson to learn from the unexpected and unknown. Nevertheless, please consider when unexpected events happen in your life that cause significant distress or pain, it may be the very thing that leads you to your purpose. Nice talking with you, my friend, take care.

Bibliography

Chapter 2

National Institute of Neurological Disorders and Stroke. "Multiple Sclerosis: Hope Through Research." Bethesda, MD: National Institutes of Health, 2020. https://catalog.ninds.nih.gov/sites/default/files/publications /multiple-sclerosis-hope-through-research_0.pdf

National Multiple Sclerosis Society. "MS Signs & Symptoms." *Symptoms & Diagnosis* (website). Accessed November 29, 2021. https://www.nationalmssociety.org/Symptoms-Diagnosis/MS-Symptoms

Chapter 3

Olesen, Jacob. "Biblical Meaning of Colors." *Colors Meanings* (blog). Jacob Olesen. Accessed November 29, 2021. https://www.color-meanings.com/biblical-meaning-colors/

About the Author

Sierra Hairston is a multiple sclerosis advocate and thriver, writer, content creator, small business owner, dancer, volunteer, and social worker. She was born in Greensboro, North Carolina. She received her Bachelor of Social Work degree from North Carolina Agricultural and Technical State University in 2013. She earned her Master of Social Work degree from the Joint Master of Social Work Program between North Carolina Agricultural and Technical State University and the University of North Carolina at Greensboro in 2015. Sierra has over five years of experience in the social work field, working in various clinical and caseworker roles.

After being diagnosed with Relapsing-Remitting Multiple Sclerosis in April 2016, Sierra's mother encouraged her to begin journaling to start her healing process. Sierra and her mother discovered her gift for writing inspirational messages through journaling. Sierra's social work background and her mother's background in nursing prompted them to combine both fields and build a service-based business.

Sierra is a proud volunteer who loves to serve and give back to the community through acts of service and kindness in person and online. She is known to educate people in the multiple sclerosis community on her wellness journey and encourage and motivate them to be their best selves. She is passionate about dancing and working out, taking photos of nature, and spending time with her family, friends, and dogs.

Connect with Sierra through her YouTube Channel, Sierra C. Hairston, and business website www.timelyfountain.com. Sierra loves to engage in the community and would love to speak at your next conference, service, podcast interview, and television interview to encourage and empower people living with or without a chronic illness to live with purpose and overcome adversity. Speaking engagement requests can be sent to info@sierrachairston.com.

www.ingramcontent.com/pod-product-compliance
Lightning Source LLC
LaVergne TN
LVHW052036080426
835513LV00018B/2352